NANABUSH TALES

THE STORY OF RACCOON

Written by Richard Nanawin
Illustrated by Yousra Zekrifa

Text copyright © 2023 by Richard Nanawin
Illustrations copyrigt © 2023 by Yousra Zekrifa

No part of this publication may be reproduced, stored in a retrieval system, or transmitted in any form recording, or otherwise, without written permission of the publisher.

Nanabush lived in a village, he'd built two lodges, one for himself and another for two very old brothers who were blind. He tied a rope from their lodge to the water's edge so they could follow the rope to get water when they needed.

One day Raccoon (Esiban) decided to play a trick on the brothers, he saw the one brother coming down the path to fetch water, Racoon quickly untied the rope and threw it up near the trees.

The brother returned to the lodge and said he couldn't find the water; the other brother took the pail and began to follow the rope to the lakes edge. Racoon saw the other brother coming, he quickly grabbed the rope and placed it back in the water

The brother found the water, retrieved some and walked back to the cabin

When brother returned, he said " your lazy brother, you wanted me to get the water", the other brother replied, " I could not find the water, I'm glad you did, let's have some tea".

As the brothers were sitting down to drink their tea, Nanabus entered their lodge and announced he'd brought them some fresh deer stew and corn, the brothers were pleased.

Nanabush made sure each brother had two pieces of deer meat in each of their bowls.

Raccoon had smelled the deer stew and followed Nanabush to the brother's lodge, after Nanabush left, Raccoon crept up upon the table, took the deer meat from one brothers bowl,

He scurried to the corner of lodge where he quickly enjoyed his fresh deer meat.

As the brothers began to eat, the one brother said, "your greedy brother, you've taken my deer meat", the other brother exclaimed " I have done no such thing, Nanabush gave us two pieces each".

When the brothers resumed eating, the other brother yelled "You took my deer meat", the other brother yelled back " I did not, you must've eaten them already". The brothers began to yell louder and began to wrestle and fight, raccoon was very happy to watch the brother fight.

Nanabush had heard the yelling and ran over the lodge to find the two-brothers wrestling on the floor, Raccoon saw Nanabush coming and tried to leave the lodge without being seen.

Nanabush saw Raccoon and grabbed him by the scuff, " What have you been up to?".

Nanabush listened to the brother's story, he was angered by Raccoon's behavior and the troubles he'd caused the brothers.

Nanabush decided the world would know of Raccoon's misery, he told Raccoon, "I am going to take away half your eyesight, you will see but not very well, you will only be able to hunt at night, when you do find food, you will have to find water to wash it before you eat".

Nanabush took some so soot from the fire and rubbed it across Raccoon's face, he took more and wiped it across Raccoon tale.

You can find Other Stories by Richard Nanawin on
Amazon.com

www.ingramcontent.com/pod-product-compliance
Lightning Source LLC
Chambersburg PA
CBRC100024110526
44587CB00007BA/160